SEA

illustrated by Lynne Cherry

Methuen Children's Books

Big seals, little seals.
Look at all the seals.

They swim. They splash.
They roll in the waves.

They dive

deep

deep

down

and then come up again to breathe.

The water is cold,
but not to a seal.
It has a sleek fur coat
to keep it warm.

A seal's home is by the sea.

for Gunvor, Steve, Synne and Kari-Anna Wing,
my good friends whose home is by the sea

First published in Great Britain in 1987
by Methuen Children's Books Ltd
11 New Fetter Lane, London EC4P 4EE

Published in the United States by E P Dutton, New York
Text copyright © 1987 E P Dutton
Illustrations copyright © 1987 Lynne Cherry

Printed in Singapore by Tien Wah Press
All rights reserved
Licensed by World Wildlife Fund

ISBN 0 416 03022 X